# I'm Thinking of a Mississippi River State

Bela Davis

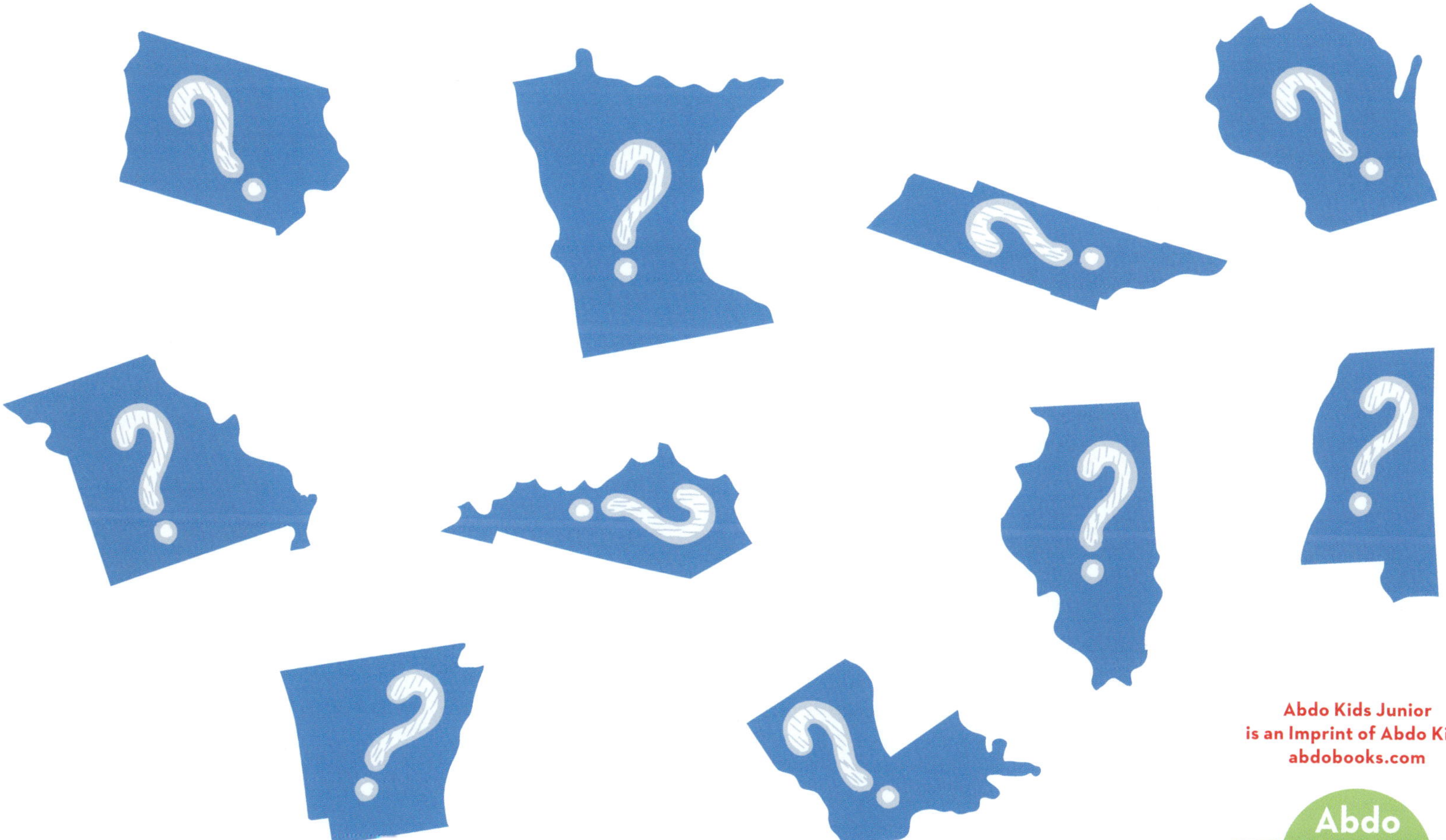

Abdo Kids Junior
is an Imprint of Abdo Kids
abdobooks.com

Abdo
I'M THINKING OF A STATE
Kids

**abdobooks.com**

Published by Abdo Kids, a division of ABDO, P.O. Box 398166, Minneapolis, Minnesota 55439.

Printed in the United States of America, North Mankato, Minnesota.

102025

012026

THIS BOOK CONTAINS RECYCLED MATERIALS

Photo Credits: Alamy, Getty Images, Shutterstock

Production Contributors: Teddy Borth, Jennie Forsberg, Grace Hansen

Design Contributors: Candice Keimig, Pakou Moua

Library of Congress Control Number: 2025936500

Publisher's Cataloging-in-Publication Data

Names: Davis, Bela, author.

Title: I'm thinking of a Mississippi river state / by Bela Davis

Description: Minneapolis, Minnesota : Abdo Kids, 2026 | Series: I'm thinking of a state | Includes online resources and index.

Identifiers: ISBN 9798384907398 (lib. bdg.) | ISBN 9798384908098 (ebook) | ISBN 9798384908449 (Read-to-Me ebook)

Subjects: LCSH: Mississippi River Valley--Juvenile literature. | American states (United States)--Juvenile literature. | Geography--Juvenile literature. | Physical geography--United States--Juvenile literature.

Classification: DDC 917--dc23

# Table of Contents

# Guess the State!

I'm thinking of a Mississippi River state! This is a state that touches the Mississippi River.

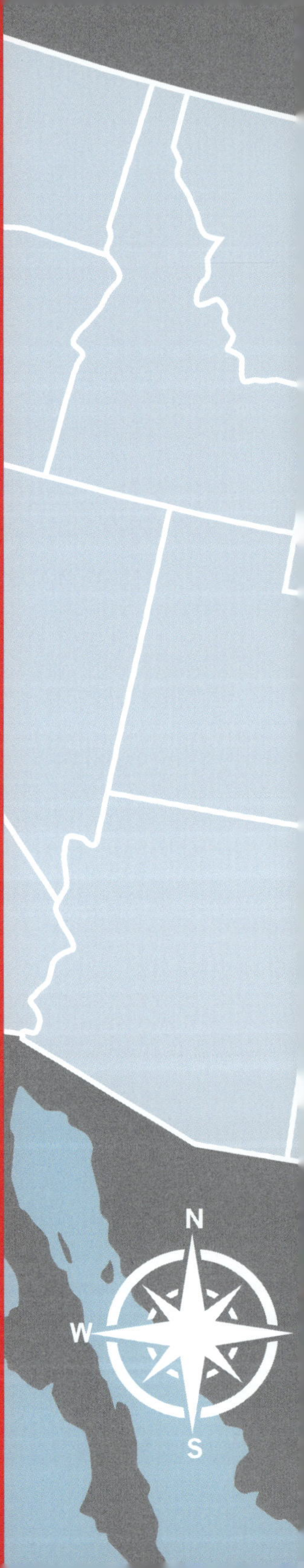

Canada
Minnesota
Wisconsin
Iowa
Illinois
Missouri
Kentucky
Tennessee
Arkansas
Mississippi
Louisiana
Mexico
Mississippi River

Can you guess the state?

The state flower is the

**showy** lady's slipper.

**State Clues**

- **Flower:** Lady's slipper

The state bird is the loon.

**State Clues**

- **Flower:** Lady's slipper
- **Bird:** Loon

Fishers can catch big walleye in this state!

**State Clues**

- **Flower:** Lady's slipper
- **Bird:** Loon
- **Animal:** Walleye

People fish here all year round. They even go ice fishing!

**State Clues**

- **Flower:** Lady's slipper
- **Bird:** Loon
- **Animal:** Walleye
- **Activity:** Ice fishing

THE
ELIMINATER

Mall of America is in this state.

It has a roller coaster inside!

**State Clues**

- **Flower:** Lady's slipper
- **Bird:** Loon
- **Animal:** Walleye
- **Activity:** Ice fishing
- **Visit:** Mall of America

People can explore and camp in Voyageurs **National Park**.

**State Clues**

| | |
|---|---|
| • **Flower:** | **Lady's slipper** |
| • **Bird:** | **Loon** |
| • **Animal:** | **Walleye** |
| • **Activity:** | **Ice fishing** |
| • **Visit:** | **Mall of America** |
| • **Explore:** | **Voyageurs** |

The state's capital is Saint Paul.

**State Clues**

- **Flower:** Lady's slipper
- **Bird:** Loon
- **Animal:** Walleye
- **Activity:** Ice fishing
- **Visit:** Mall of America
- **Explore:** Voyageurs
- **Capital:** Saint Paul

Now you have all the clues! Can you guess what state I'm thinking of?

**State Clues**

- **Flower:** Lady's slipper
- **Bird:** Loon
- **Animal:** Walleye
- **Activity:** Ice fishing
- **Visit:** Mall of America
- **Explore:** Voyageurs
- **Capital:** Saint Paul

IL
MS
MN
IA

# I'm Thinking of...
# Minnesota!

# Glossary

**national park**
a special area of land that is set aside by the United States government to protect it.

**showy**
bright, colorful, and grand in appearance.

# Index